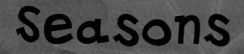

Seasons

Autumn

Monica Hughes

Raintree

www.raintreepublishers.co.uk
Visit our website to find out more information about **Raintree** books.

To order:
☎ Phone 44 (0) 1865 888112
▤ Send a fax to 44 (0) 1865 314091
▭ Visit the Raintree Bookshop at **www.raintreepublishers.co.uk** to browse our catalogue and order online.

First published in Great Britain by Raintree, Halley Court, Jordan Hill, Oxford OX2 8EJ, part of Harcourt Education.
Raintree is a registered trademark of Harcourt Education Ltd.

Editorial: Charlotte Guillain and Diyan Leake
Design: Michelle Lisseter
Picture Research: Maria Joannou and Liz Savery
Production: Lorraine Hicks

Originated by Dot Gradations
Printed and bound in China by
South China Printing Company

ISBN 1 844 21339 0 (hardback)
ISBN 978 1 844 21339 9 (hardback)
07 06 05 04
10 9 8 7 6 5 4 3 2

ISBN 1 844 21344 7 (paperback)
ISBN 978 1 844 21344 3 (paperback)
08
10 9 8 7 6

British Library Cataloguing in Publication Data
Hughes, Monica
Autumn
508.2
A full catalogue record for this book is available from the British Library.

Acknowledgements
The publishers would like to thank the following for permission to reproduce photographs: Bruce Coleman Collection pp. **16**, **19** (Robert Maier), **23h**; Bubbles pp. **9**, **20**, **23f**; FLPA (Catherine Mullen) p. **23b**; Getty Images p. **21**; Holt Studios International pp. **12**, **15**, **23e**, **23g**; Mark Boulton pp. **11**, **13**, **14**, **23a**, **23c**; NHPA (Manfred Danegger) p. **17**; Getty Images/Stone p. **7**; Retna Pictures p. **8** Sally & Richard Greenhill Library p. **10**; Trevor Clifford p. **4**; Tudor Photography p. **22**; Woodfall Wild Images pp. **5**, **6**, **18**, **23d**.

Cover photograph of trees in autumn, reproduced with permission of Photodisc.

Every effort has been made to contact copyright holders of any material reproduced in this book. Any omissions will be rectified in subsequent printings if notice is given to the publishers.

Contents

Some words are shown in bold, **like this**. You can find them in the glossary on page 23.

When is autumn?

It is never clear when one season ends and the next one begins.

Autumn is the season after summer and before winter.

We say that autumn starts on 21 September.

September, October and November are the autumn months.

What is the weather like in autumn?

Autumn is colder than summer but warmer than winter.

Mornings are often **misty** and there may be **frost** on the grass.

Often there are strong winds.

Sometimes there are thunderstorms.

What happens in towns in autumn?

There are lots of fallen leaves everywhere.

It is hard work clearing them all away.

Shops show all the things you need for the start of the new school year.

What happens in the country in autumn?

Farmers harvest the last crops.

They **plough** the fields ready for the next season.

There are lots of fruit and
vegetables to sell at the market.

What foods do we eat in autumn?

Wild blackberries in **hedgerows** become **ripe**.

It is fun to pick and eat them.

Lots of different fruit and vegetables are ripe and ready to eat.

What happens to animals in autumn?

There are lots of nuts and berries to eat.

Squirrels collect nuts and **store** them ready to eat in the winter.

Some birds prepare to fly to warmer places as the weather gets colder.

What happens to plants in autumn?

The leaves of many trees change colour in the autumn.

They go from green to orange, red, brown, yellow, gold and even purple.

There are nuts, seeds and cones on many trees.

Garden flowers begin to die after the first **frosts**.

What celebrations take place in autumn?

There are harvest festival displays in schools and churches.

Halloween takes place on 31 October.

Bonfires and sparklers are part of the fun on 5 November.

Divali is also celebrated with lights and fireworks.

Make an autumn leaf print

Paint the underside of some leaves with thick paint.

Carefully press the painted side onto your paper.

Lift off the leaf to see your print.

Glossary

anorak
warm jacket with a hood

frost
thin, powdery ice

hedgerow
bushes growing close together in a row

misty
foggy and hazy, not clear

plough
use a machine to turn over soil to get it ready for planting

reflective
shows up and shines in lights

ripe
ready to be picked and eaten

store
put away until needed

Index